Windows 10

The Ultimate Beginner's Manual

By Max Green

Table of Contents

Introduction

I want to thank you and congratulate you for downloading the book, *Windows 10: The Ultimate Beginner's Manual.* This book contains proven steps and strategies on how to prepare for the upgrade to Windows 10 to best ensure that you come through the process with all of your files and programs intact.

The following chapters will discuss what to expect when switching from Windows 7 and 8 to Windows 10, and the most efficient ways of doing so while still retaining the option to switch back to your previous operating system if you change your mind. Windows 10 gives you a month to decide before locking you in but if you follow the plan listed in the following chapters you will be able to bail out whenever you like.

Finally, it ends with a discussion of common questions users have after upgrading as well as a solution or two for each that tends to work most of the time. Many of these questions include answers which involve speeding up routine OS functions and as such may be worth a look even if your Windows 10 experience has been largely trouble free so far.

Thanks again for downloading this book, I hope you enjoy it!

Chapter 1: Windows 10 versus Windows 7 and 8

Microsoft's latest OS is here and they are giving it away for free to Windows 7 and 8 users who download it before August 2016. Just because it's free however, doesn't necessarily mean that you should run right out and download it. This chapter will discuss the main difference between Windows 7 and 8 and Windows 10 so you can make an educated decision as to whether or not to click Upgrade Now the next time the offer appears on your screen.

Performance

All other things being equal, Windows 10 boots up much more quickly from a powered down state than Windows 7 and also faster than Windows 8. In addition, hardware acceleration has been improved over both versions so the general experience of navigating around the OS feels smother as well. Upgrading on a laptop or tablet will also result in improved battery life though not by a large degree.

When it comes to gaming, the various operating systems perform about the same but Windows 10 boasts access to the newest version of DirectX 12 which it says will only be available on its newest OS. DirectX is a piece of software that interacts with games and the hardware they run on to improve performance and allow developers to squeeze the most out of the hardware. DirectX 12 offers a low-level hardware abstraction which comes in the form of an enhancement to Direct3D which will allow developers a greater opportunity to optimize their games with specific hardware in mind.

DirectX 12 also improves on the draw call overhead of previous versions which up until this point had been a limiting factor to how many objects could be seen onscreen at one time. Another major improvement to DirectX 12 is its multi-adapter capabilities which means that games will now be able to use multiple graphics cards at once regardless of each individual card's speed or brand. Taken as a whole these changes will mean that more and more developers will soon be taking advantage of DirectX 12 and users interested in benefiting from these changes will be forced to follow suit.

Design

Windows 8 debuted with a drastically redesigned interface that was divisive to say the least. It moved away from the Window's 7 model of transparent windows and detailed iconography to flat icons and bold colors. It also featured an interface that skewed heavily towards touch interfaces. Windows 10 takes cues from both systems with desktop icons receiving a new flat and colorful designs while other core features retain their old Windows 7 look. User's also have the option of making windows transparent or solid depending on their UI preferences.

As far as the interface goes, there is a little bit of Windows 8 here and there but by and large Microsoft took the time to ensure that the new interface works as well with a keyboard and mouse as it does with touch commands. This is possible thanks to what Microsoft refers to as a "continuum" model. This means that essentially all the versions of Windows 10 are the same, the OS simply determines what hardware it is currently running on and adapts accordingly. For example, if you are using a tablet with a connected keyboard then Windows 10 will run in standard Home or Professional mode; remove the keyboard however, and Windows 10 will switch to the mobile version of the OS and activate functions such as touch-specific inputs.

Start menu

The Windows 10 Start menu is perhaps the place the new OS blends the previous two the most, though user's have the option to customize it as much as they like. The left side of the menu is reminiscent of the start menu that Windows 8 initially removed to a general outcry of dismay. It contains frequently accessed programs (now called applications) access to core functions such as settings and power options and an expanded search function which searches for websites as well as local instances of the search topic. The search function is connected to Cortana, Microsoft's voice activated search aid as well.

The right side of the Start menu looks like a smaller version of Windows 8 Live Tiles system with users able to pin any application to the menu, some of which provide continuously updating information. These tiles can be extensively customized or turned off entirely based on personal preference. The most notable omission from the Start menu is a lack of quick access to the control panel.

File management

Windows 8 improved on the Windows 7 approach to file management and Windows 10 takes those improvements a step further. Windows 10 has added the Up button back in the File Explorer option which those who have been using Windows for several iterations will be glad to see once again when navigating file paths. Windows 10 takes its cues from Windows 8 when it comes to the top menu ribbon with all the most used tools easily and readily available. The addition of a selection of sharing options also makes moving files between programs including Skype, Dropbox and Outlook much more simple.

Another major improvement over previous versions of Windows currently available in Windows 10 is the redesigned file copying interface. Previous copying and moving items were considered different task but now they are collected into a single window for easier management. What's more, transfer speeds are now shown in real time and they can be paused or canceled instead of simply canceled.

Perhaps the biggest improvement to the way files are managed is the new Storage Spaces management system. This option provides a way for users to group several hard drives together to form one logical drive. This will increase redundancy and ensure that data is backed up more securely than previous versions of Windows could manage.

Multiple Monitor Support

Windows 10 improves upon previous OS iterations when it comes to supporting multiple monitors as well. Windows 7 and 8 offered minimal multi-monitor support and snapping options while Windows 10 beefs up these features substantially. Multiple monitors can now each have a unique taskbar and snapping has been expanded to all four quadrants of the screen. What's more, Windows 10 now offers users the ability to create virtual desktops and switch between them with Windows Key + Tab.

Chapter 2: Preparing for and Upgrading to Windows 10

Once you have looked over the changes Windows 10 promises and decided that they offer functions you will find useful, the next step is to prepare your computer for the upgrade process and install Windows 10. Unlike previous versions of Windows, Windows 10 was designed from the start to run on a wide variety of devices. Anyone using Windows 7 or Windows 8 will be able to upgrade to Windows 10 for free until August 2016. Once the free installation window has expired, Windows 10 Home will retail for $120, Windows 10 Professional will cost $199 and to upgrade from one to the other will cost $99.

Prepare to Upgrade

Check compatibility

Microsoft has made upgrading to Windows 10 a fairly straightforward process, and most of your settings, files and applications will be moved over without issue. This is not the case for every program or file however so you should run the Windows 10 Upgrade Advisor before you decide to upgrade. This program will scan your current setup and determine which programs or drivers (if any) are not currently available for Windows 10.

Some features that will be lost include Windows 7 desktop gadgets, some forms of virus software, and any child safety settings previously set. In addition, Windows Media Center will be removed on upgrade though a new application, Windows DVD Player will automatically install for a limited time, after that it will be available in the Windows Store. Minesweeper, Solitaire and Hearts will all be removed, Microsoft versions of those games are available in the store. Windows 10 does not currently have MDM functionality.

Create a recovery drive and back up personal files

Windows 10 gives users the opportunity to revert to their old OS for the first month after upgrading but just in case, it is best to create a recovery drive on the off chance you come across a crippling problem without another solution. Before you upgrade, running the Windows Recovery Tool, is a good idea, just in case. Take note, this drive will contain the basic Windows installation files, drives and original shipping hardware, you should back up all your personal files separately.

Create a Microsoft ID

The newest version of Windows has increased cloud functionality to allow users to seamlessly transfer their experience from one platform to another. As a result, it contains heavy integration with a user's Microsoft Account (this functionality can be curtailed by simply creating a local Microsoft Account on your current system). Already having a preexisting

Microsoft ID is not officially listed as a requirement for upgrading but not entering an ID when prompted has been known to cause upgrade issues in some users. Creating a Microsoft Account can be done from the settings menu by clicking on Change my PC Settings and clicking on Accounts then My Accounts, you will then have the option of associating your system with an existing account or to create a new one.

Windows Hello

Users switching from Windows 8.1 with hardware which contains a RealSense 3D camera or biometric scanning capabilities can go ahead and activate additional security features that will allow them to bypass the traditional login screen. This feature is called Windows Hello and can be activated by visiting Settings, then Accounts, then Sign-In Options.

Upgrading

Hardware Requirements

The installation requirements of the PC version of Windows 10 requires the following minimum system components.

- The most recent version of Windows 7 or Windows 8 must be installed
- A processor 1 GHz or faster
- 1 gigabyte of ram for 32-bit systems or 2 gigabytes for 64-bit systems

- A 32-bit version of the OS will require 16 gigabytes of space and the 64-bit version will require 20 gigabytes of space
- A video card compatible with at least DirectX 9
- A display which is capable of producing at least 800x600 pixels.
- An internet connection capable of downloading three gigabytes of data.
- Eligible personal computers and laptops have a Windows 10 upgrade button added to their taskbar

Hardware requirements for the mobile version of Windows 10 include

- At least 512 megabytes of available memory
- Four gigabytes of free storage space
- A phone which supports DirectX 9
- A power, volume, start and back button
- Four gigabytes of memory if your screen has a resolution of 2560x2048
- Three gigabytes of memory if your screen has a resolution of 2560x1600 or 2048x1152
- Two gigabytes of memory if your screen has a resolution of 1920x1080, 1920x1200 or 1440x900

One gigabyte of memory for any lower screen resolutions all the way down to 800x480

Once you have taken the time to ensure that your upgrade to Windows 10 goes as smoothly as possible it is time to click on the Windows 10 icon already in the notification section of your taskbar. Clicking get started will allow you to reserve your copy of Windows 10 from Microsoft. Reserving your copy should begin the download process but if it doesn't open Windows Update (easily found by typing the name into your search bar) and the upgrade should be in the resulting menu waiting for you. Clicking on this option will download Windows 10 over your existing OS. It is also possible to initiate a clean install of Windows 10 if you do not wish to save any of your settings and in turn plan to erase your hard drive beforehand.

Perform a Clean Install

1. Ensure you have your Windows 10 product key and a flash drive with at least four gigabytes of free space. Your product key can be found in the confirmation email you received when you confirmed your upgrade.
2. Go online visit Microsoft.com and search for Windows 10 ISO. This will let you download the tools required to create a copy of the installation data.
3. Visit Rufus.akeo.ie and download the software you find there; this will let you transfer the data you downloaded from Microsoft.com to your flash drive.
4. Insert the flash drive into your computer and run the program you downloaded from Rufus.akeo.ie and select the Create a Bootable Disk option.
5. Once the file has finished transferring, reboot your computer and press F12 (F2

if F12 doesn't work) when the
manufacturer logo appears on the
screen. Select boot from install disk
when given the option and the Windows
10 installation menu should appear.
6. Select a language and then if you are
interested in a clean install, click on the
custom option.
7. Delete your current partitions and then
select the Unallocated space option
8. Let the installation commence, enter
your product key when prompted.

Installation Issues

If you are attempting to update from Windows
7 or Windows 8 to Windows 10 before August
of 2016 and you are not given the option to
automatically update to Windows 10 then the
following trouble shooting tips might help.

Start by determining if Windows Update is
installing updates automatically.

1. Start by searching for Windows Update
and opening the result
2. Click on Choose How Updates Get
Installed and then choose the option
under Important Updates
3. Select the option to install
recommended updates the say way
important updates are installed.
4. Select the option for Microsoft Update
and select Give Me Updates for Other
Microsoft Products When I Update
Windows and click apply.

5. Open the Command Prompt in Administrator Mode and type wuaucit.exe/updatenow
6. Your download should begin

Dual Boot Windows 10

If you are not completely sold on the idea of upgrading to Windows 10 but you want to see what you are missing, you can install it alongside your current operating system.

1. Ensure your computer has enough hard drive space to allow for the additional OS.
2. Follow the previous steps to create a flash drive version of the Windows 10 installation file.
3. Create a new partition on your hard drive by opening the command prompt and typing diskmgmt.msc
4. Right click on an area of free space and then click on New Simple Volume follow the resulting steps, being sure to set the size of the new partition in megabytes.
5. Follow the rest of the steps and then use the Format Partition option to finish creating the new partition (the default selections should be fine)
6. With the partition created it is time to reboot your computer and select the boot drive as detailed above. When asked, select custom installation and choose the newly created partition.

7. When booting the computer simply select which OS to boot but remember there will be no crossover between the files in the two different partitions.

Delete your Old OS

Once you have tried out Windows 10 for long enough that you are sure you will not need to revert to your old OS it can be a good idea to delete the former OS files to free up hard drive space.

1. Search for the Disk Cleanup Utility and open the result
2. Select the option to Clean Up System Files in the lower left hand corner of the screen.
3. Choose the partition which holds your old OS (typically the OS C: Drive)
4. Find the item label Previous Windows Installations and select the option to delete it. This action will generally recover between twelve and twenty gigabytes of space.

Chapter 3: Common Questions

Why did my printer stop working after the upgrade?

If you are having trouble connecting to your printer since the upgrade a simple fix is to uninstall your printer drivers and reinstall them. To do this first open the Control Panel, then choose Devices and Printers from the available options, finally right click on your printer and choose the option to remove it. Once that is finished find the website for the company that makes your printer and find the drivers for your specific model of printer. They do not necessarily need to be Windows 10 drivers, just the most up to date drivers will do.

Why am I low on virtual memory?

Another common issue that Windows 10 users are experiencing is one that manifests itself by creating performance issues. By default, Windows 10 does not allocate as much RAM to virtual memory as previous versions of Windows, instead relying on computers with more RAM to pick up the slack.

If your computer is running slow after the upgrade simply go to the Control Panel and search for Performance. Now select the Adjust the Appearance and Performance of Windows option then select Advanced Options. Select Change from the virtual Memory options and then deselect the box for the option to Automatically manage Paging File Size. Finally, select the Windows 10 drive (most likely C:) and choose the option to set a different size and then alter the maximum and initial size options to the values Windows recommends. Choose OK and restart your computer.

Why are my files using the wrong files to open after the update?

After updating to Windows 10 many users find that some of their commonly used file types are now opening with the help of different programs. This is either the case because the program you previously used did not make the transition to Windows 10 because a compatible version was not yet available or because you previously changed the default program that file type opens with and it has now been reset to the default.

When you come across a file that is behaving in this manner all you need to do is right-click on it and choose the Open With option. Next select the Choose Another App option and select the application (what programs are now called) you would like to use to open the file type instead. Choose the Always Use This App option and then select OK.

Why can't I find my favorites in Microsoft Edge

When you first load up Windows 10 one of the most extensive changes you will find come in the form of the entirely redesign web browser call Microsoft Edge. If after you upgrade, you are having trouble finding your favorites from Internet Explorer or just want to import your bookmarks from another browser then follow these steps. Select the menu option which looks like three individual lines and then choose the Import Favorites Option. Select the browser from which you wish to import your favorites and then select the Import option.

Why does it take so long for Windows to boot?

Too many applications

If after you upgrade to Windows 10 you find that the amount of time it takes for the OS to cold boot seems to get longer and longer then you may need to decrease the number of applications that automatically start each time you boot your computer. To change the applications that start when the computer does simple search for the Task Manger and then open it. Select the More Details option followed by the Start-Up tab at the top of the window. Next choose the Status column and determine that you want to see which applications start automatically. When you find an application you do not want to start automatically check the option to disable it. Reboot your computer and view the results.

Too many services

It is also possible to determine which services that run automatically in the background while your computer is active are also unnecessary and by so doing free up a substantial amount of your OS's resources. First you will need to open the Services Manager window, you can do this by pressing the Windows Key + X to access the quick access menu before selecting the option for Computer Management. Select the Services and Applications option from the resulting window. You can also go you My Computer and select the manage option or right-clicking on the This PC icon on the desktop.

In the Services Manager you will see a wide variety of all the services which are currently active or inactive on your device. The section of the window labeled Status will show you if a service is currently active. When deciding which services to prevent from starting automatically always set them to Manual and never disabled as this will allow Windows to continue to turn the service on when it needs to use it.

Services which can be set to manual

- **Connected User Experiences and Telemetry:** Everyone should turn this off regardless of system usage as it prevents Microsoft from collecting and monitoring your data.
- **DMWApPushSVC:** Set this to off to prevent telemetry and data collection

- **Diagnostic Tracking Service**: Turn this off to prevent telemetry and data collection
- Diagnostic Policy Service
- Windows Search (if you don't use this feature)
- Windows Image Acquisition or WIA (if you do not have a scanner)
- Windows Error Reporting Service
- Windows Defender (if you have other virus software)
- Touch Keyboard and Handwriting Panel Service (assuming you don't use these features)
- TCP/IP NetBIOS Helper (if you are not connected to a workgroup network)
- Security Center
- Secondary Logon
- Remote Registry (Set this to disabled to increase security)
- Print Spooler (if you do not have a printer)
- Program Compatibility Assistant Service
- IP Helper (If you do not use your IPv6 connection)
- Downloaded Maps Manager (if you do not use the maps application)
- Distributed Link Tracking Client (if you do not connect through a network)

Too much eye candy

In its default state Windows 10 contains a wide variety of animations and effects to add a little extra visual flair to the user interface. If you find yourself experiencing slowdown as you move through routine Windows 10 functions, then tweaking these visual enhancements may improve your performance. To begin, press the Windows key + R to open the Run command line. Next time in sysdm.cpl and press the Enter key. Next open the Advanced options before selecting Settings which can be found under the Performance heading.

When a new window opens uncheck the some or all of the properties listed below:

- Use drop shadows
- Scroll boxes smoothly
- Slide combo boxes open
- When making a selection show a selection rectangle
- Show windows with shadows
- Show the mouse pointer with shadows
- Save thumbnail previews from the taskbar
- Clicking on a menu item fades it out
- Determine how tooltips appear
- Determine how menus appear
- Determine the level of animation in the taskbar
- Determine the level of window animation occurs when maximizing or minimizing a window
- Determine the level of animation seen on elements and control available inside windows

When you have made your selections choose the option to apply the changes and close the window. If you are instead interested in switching all of the Windows 10 animations off at once you can instead press the Windows key + I before choosing the Ease of Action Menu from the Other Options tab. Then choose the Play Animations in Windows Option and set it to off.

You can also choose to disable the transparency effects visible on the Start menu, Action Center and taskbar. To do this, open the setting application from the start menu and choose the personalization option. Next select the options for Colors and choose the option to Make Start, Action Center and Taskbar Transparent. Set this to off and apply settings before closing the window.

Too many folder options

If you find that your performance slows while you are searching through folders, then turning off some of the folder features you do not use can increase performance. To do this first open the This PC application found on the desktop before choosing View from the resulting options. Next choose the options selection to open Folder Options. Next choose the View tab and look through the options presented. Choose the ones you do not use and uncheck those boxes. Click apply and close the window.

Why does Windows 10 update automatically?

With Windows 10 Microsoft has by default taken away the user's ability to determine whether or not they want to install software updates. While you cannot disable this decision, you can easily create a restore point for your system in case the new updates don't play well with your computer. Simply search for System Protection, start the application and follow the onscreen instructions.

Do I have to sign in every time?

Windows 10 has significantly increased its integration with the Microsoft Account which in turn requires a password every time you start your computer. First press the Windows Key + R to open the run command line. Next type netpllwiz and hit the Enter key. Then choose a user account you want Windows to sign into automatically at startup and deselect the Users Must Enter Username option. Finally, enter your password in the Automatically Log On box and click OK.

How do I change the default Windows 10 sounds?

If you do not enjoy the default sounds that come with Windows 10 you can easily change them by first pressing the Windows key + X to bring up the Control Panel. Next choose the sound icon (this can be reached directly by opening the Run command line and typing mmsys.cpl and hitting enter). Now choose Sounds from the presented options, this will show you a list of all of the actions that result in a sound. You can change them individually or explore the many themes available. Click apply to save your changes before closing the window.

How do I bring back classic programs?

If, once you have explored Windows 10 you decide you just don't like all these new-fangled applications and want to bring back your favorite programs instead, it can be a little tricky but it is possible. Before finding your old favorites, you will need to uninstall the new applications which can be tricky as there is no simple way to remove these applications. First you must download the program CCleaner from PiriForm.com/CCleaner/download, this program is a simple and free way to remove temporary files from your computer and to thereby improve system performance. Version 5.11 of CCleaner now allows users to remove built-in Windows 10 applications. Once you have downloaded and installed CCleaner, run the program and in the Tools tab you will find an option to uninstall applications.

If you would rather simply uninstall all of the preinstalled applications, you can remove them all at once without having to download any third party software. This is done by using a program called PowerShell that is part of the basic Windows 10 installation. To access PowerShell simply search for it from the Start menu. Before you click on the program hold down Ctrl + Shift + Enter to start the program in administrator mode. Right-clicking on the program and selecting the Run as Administrator choice is also an option.

While this screen may look intimidating the ways you have to interact with it are fairly linear. If you plan on uninstalling all of the installed applications for all users simply type Get-AppxPackage followed by Remove-AppxPackage. If you would like to only remove the applications from a single user, simply type Get-AppxPackage-user *username* followed by Remove-AppxPackage. Removing all of the installed applications is not recommended in most cases as it can affect functionality in unexpected ways.

If you would like to uninstall individual applications using the PowerShell method as opposed to the CCleaner method use the following list of commands.

- *To uninstall the Messaging and Skype Video applications:* Get-AppxPackage* messaging* then Remove-AppxPackage
- *To uninstall the Sway application:* Get-AppxPackage*sway* then Remove-AppxPackage
- *To uninstall the Sway application:* Get-AppxPackage*sway* then Remove-AppxPackage
- *To uninstall the Phone application:* Get-AppxPackage*commsphone* then Remove-AppxPackage
- *To uninstall the Phone Companion application:* Get-

AppxPackage*windowsphone* then
Remove-AppxPackage

- *To uninstall the Phone and Phone
  Companion applications:* Get-
  AppxPackage*phone* then Remove-
  AppxPackage
- *To uninstall the Calendar and Mail
  applications:* Get-
  AppxPackage*communicationsapps*
  then Remove-AppxPackage
- *To uninstall the People application:*
  Get-AppxPackage*people* then
  Remove-AppxPackage
- *To uninstall the Groove Music
  application:* Get-
  AppxPackage*zunemusic* then
  Remove-AppxPackage
- *To uninstall the Movies and Television
  application:* Get-
  AppxPackage*zunevideo* then Remove-
  AppxPackage
- *To uninstall the Groove Music and
  Movies and television applications:*
  Get-AppxPackage*zune* then Remove-
  AppxPackage
- *To uninstall the Money application:*
  Get-AppxPackage*bingfinance* then
  Remove-AppxPackage
- *To uninstall the News application:* Get-
  AppxPackage*bingnews* then Remove-
  AppxPackage
- *To uninstall the Sports application:*
  Get-AppxPackage*bingsports* then
  Remove-AppxPackage

- *To uninstall the Weather application:* Get-AppxPackage*bingweather* then Remove-AppxPackage
- *To uninstall the Money, News Weather and Sports applications:* Get-AppxPackage*bing* then Remove-AppxPackage
- *To uninstall the OneNote application:* Get-AppxPackage*onenote* then Remove-AppxPackage
- *To uninstall the Alarms & Clock application:* Get-AppxPackage*alarms* then Remove-AppxPackage
- *To uninstall the Calculator application:* Get-AppxPackage*calculator* then Remove-AppxPackage
- *To uninstall the Camera application:* Get-AppxPackage*camera* then Remove-AppxPackage
- *To uninstall the Photos application:* Get-AppxPackage*photos* then Remove-AppxPackage
- *To uninstall the Maps application:* Get-AppxPackage*maps* then Remove-AppxPackage
- *To uninstall the Voice Recorder application:* Get-AppxPackage*soundrecorder* then Remove-AppxPackage
- *To uninstall the Xbox application:* Get-AppxPackage*xbox* then Remove-AppxPackage
- *To uninstall the Microsoft Solitaire Collection application:* Get-AppxPackage*solitaire* then Remove-AppxPackage

- *To uninstall the Office application:* Get-AppxPackage*officehub then Remove-AppxPackage
- *To uninstall the Skype application:* Get-AppxPackage*skypeapp* then Remove-AppxPackage
- *To uninstall the Get Started application:* Get-AppxPackage*getstarted* then Remove-AppxPackage
- *To uninstall the 3D Builder application:* Get-AppxPackage*3dbuilder* then Remove-AppxPackage
- *To uninstall the Windows Store application:* Get-AppxPackage*windowsstore* then Remove-AppxPackage (not recommended)

Once you have removed all of the applications you deem unnecessary you can use the following methods to find the classic versions of Microsoft programs. If there is another program out there that isn't listed that you absolutely cannot live without, don't lose hope. Odds are you are not the only one who missed that particular program and a quick web search will return a download link.

- *Classic calculator (choose classic mode):* Visit Microsoft.com and search for Calculator Plus the file is for Windows XP but it still works in Windows 10.
- *Classic MS Paint and Wordpad:* This is only possible if you have the previous

version of Windows still on your computer. Open the following file in the RUN command line C:\Windows\System 32 and press enter. Search for either the mspaint.exe or the wordpad.exe.

- *Internet Explorer:* Click on All apps followed by Windows Accessories followed by the Internet Explorer Shortcut.
- *Windows Photo Viewer:* If you upgraded to Windows 10 from Windows 7 or 8.1 you will be able to access Windows Photo Viewer by simply right-clicking on a photo and selecting Default Apps followed by Set Default Program.

Conclusion

Thank you again for reading this book! I hope it was able to help you understand what to expect when switching from Windows 7 or Windows 8 to Windows 10 and ensure that you weren't caught by surprise when making the jump to the new OS. Most importantly, I hope it was able to answer many of the common questions users have when working with Windows 10.

The next step is to either decide whether or not to upgrade to Windows 10 or if you have already upgraded then to try some of the suggested tips to make your new OS run faster and consume fewer system resources than ever before.

Finally, if you enjoyed this book, then I'd like to ask you for a favor, would you be kind enough to leave a review for this book on Amazon? It'd be greatly appreciated!

CPSIA information can be obtained at www.ICGtesting.com
Printed in the USA
LVOW10s1843050716

495171LV00020B/1394/P